71961717 ✓

||| || ||||||| || ||| | ||| ||||||||||| || |||
✍ **W9-BMO-571**

WITHDRAWN

BEING FEMALE **IN AMERICA**

SEXISM **IN POLITICS**

BY DUCHESS HARRIS, JD, PHD
WITH CHRISTINE ZUCHORA-WALSKE

Essential Library

An Imprint of Abdo Publishing | abdopublishing.com

ABDOPUBLISHING.COM

Published by Abdo Publishing, a division of ABDO, PO Box 398166, Minneapolis, Minnesota 55439. Copyright © 2018 by Abdo Consulting Group, Inc. International copyrights reserved in all countries. No part of this book may be reproduced in any form without written permission from the publisher. Essential Library™ is a trademark and logo of Abdo Publishing.

Printed in the United States of America, North Mankato, Minnesota
092017
012018

THIS BOOK CONTAINS
RECYCLED MATERIALS

Cover Photo: Dan Kosmayer/Shutterstock Images
Interior Photos: Matt Rourke/AP Images, 4–5; Julie Jacobson/AP Images, 11; North Wind Picture Archives, 14–15; Library of Congress, 21; Bettmann/Getty Images, 25; Edmonston/Records of the National Woman's Party/Library of Congress, 27; National Photo Company Collection/Library of Congress, 30–31; Charles Gorry/AP Images, 34–35; John Olson/The LIFE Picture Collection/Getty Images, 38–39; Tom Williams/CQ Roll Call/AP Images, 42–43; Shutterstock Images, 46; Charlie Neibergall/AP Images, 50–51; Seth Wenig/AP Images, 53; Zach Gibson/AP Images, 55; Scott Sonner/AP Images, 59; Andrew Lichtenstein/Corbis News/Getty Images, 60–61; Sait Serkan Gurbuz/AP Images, 64; Michael Jung/Shutterstock Images, 67; John Locher/AP Images, 70–71; Pat Benic/picture-alliance/dpa/AP Images, 76; Bill Clark/CQ Roll Call/AP Images, 78; Gregory Rec/Portland Press Herald/Getty Images, 80–81; Damian Dovarganes/AP Images, 85; Andrew Harnik/AP Images, 88–89; Erik Verduzco/Las Vegas Review-Journal/AP Images, 92–93; Alex Milan Tracy/Sipa USA/AP Images, 98

Editor: Amanda Lanser
Series Designer: Maggie Villaume

PUBLISHER'S CATALOGING-IN-PUBLICATION DATA

Names: Harris, Duchess, author | Zuchora-Walske, Christine, author.
Title: Sexism in politics / by Duchess Harris and Christine Zuchora-Walske.
Description: Minneapolis, Minnesota : Abdo Publishing, 2018. | Series: Being female in America
Identifiers: LCCN 2017946734 | ISBN 9781532113109 (lib.bdg.) | ISBN 9781532151989 (ebook)
Subjects: LCSH: Sexism--Juvenile literature. | United States--Politics and government--Juvenile literature. | Social history--Juvenile literature.
Classification: DDC 323.3--dc23
LC record available at https://lccn.loc.gov/2017946734

CONTENTS

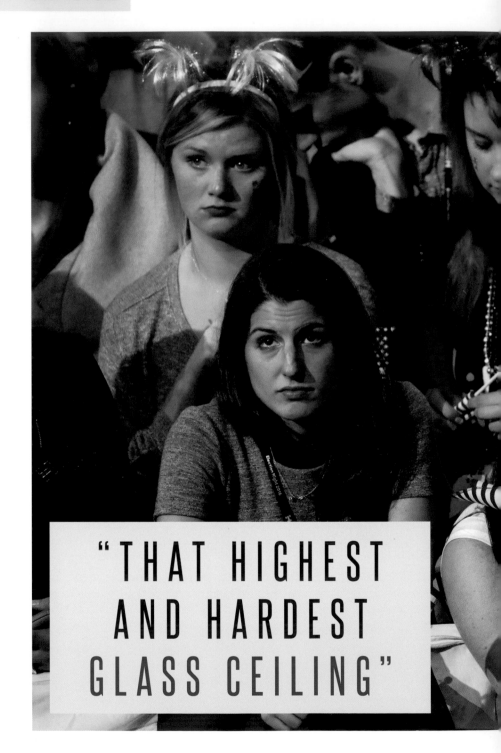

"THAT HIGHEST AND HARDEST GLASS CEILING"

It was November 8, 2016: Election Day in the United States. It had been an exhausting couple of years for everyone—candidates, campaign workers, journalists, and the American people. Finally, it was time to vote.

Ballots throughout the United States included a wide variety of issues and candidates, from tax referenda and judicial seats to state representatives and US senators. But one particular race stole the spotlight: the race for president of the United States. The two candidates were Democrat Hillary Clinton and Republican Donald Trump. Both were unusual presidential hopefuls. Trump was a billionaire real estate mogul and reality television star. Clinton was the first woman to win a major political party's presidential nomination.

HIGH HOPES

Clinton was not the first woman to run for US president. Several women had done so before her. But none had made it as far as she had. This was also not her first run at the job. In 2008, she lost the Democratic Party's nomination to Barack Obama. After her loss, she told her supporters, "Although we weren't able to shatter that highest, hardest glass ceiling this time, thanks to you, it's got about 18 million cracks in it, and the light is shining through like never before, filling us all with the hope and the sure knowledge that the path will be a little easier next time."[1]

"Next time" had arrived. And the race was looking positive for Clinton. Most political pollsters, pundits, strategists, and other experts were predicting an easy win for Clinton. A candidate needs 270 electoral votes to win the presidency. Polls projected Clinton would win at least 300.[2] In voting booths throughout the nation, her supporters voted for her gleefully, wearing pantsuits in her honor.

Then people gathered around televisions, radios, computers, and mobile devices to watch the results come in. The Trump campaign hosted a party at the Hilton Hotel in midtown Manhattan in New

York City. Clinton's party was directly across town at the Jacob K. Javits Convention Center, chosen specifically for its glass ceiling. Trump supporters were subdued. Clinton supporters were happy and expectant.

MOOD SWING

At 7:00 p.m. Eastern time, polls started closing in the eastern states. New York and Florida each have 29 electoral votes, the most for states on the East Coast. As New York was a reliable Democratic stronghold, all eyes were on Florida. Trump's campaign considered it a must-win state. Meanwhile, Clinton's campaign was confident she would win Florida. Staffers believed they had turned out a huge number of Latino voters, most of whom supported Clinton.

That confidence turned out to be misplaced. As the eastern polls closed and votes were counted, Florida became a toss-up. By 9:00 p.m., it was clear Trump would win Florida's electoral votes. This did not mean Trump would win the election. But it did suggest experts' predictions might be off. If they had been wrong about Florida, they could have made other mistakes, too. The mood at the Hilton brightened. The mood at the Javits dimmed.

The night brought more and more surprises—happy ones for the Trump team and disappointing ones for the Clinton team. As more polls closed across the country and votes were counted, Trump's chance of winning changed from hopeless to possible to likely. At the Hilton, a raucous celebration broke out. At the Javits, anxiety turned to despair and grief. After midnight, one by one, the major news organizations named Trump the winner. At 2:30 a.m., Clinton phoned Trump to concede the race.

A BITTER PILL

Many Americans stayed up all night from November 8 to November 9, 2016, to watch the election results come in. Others went to bed either hopeful or

THE US ELECTORAL SYSTEM

The US president is not determined by popular vote, or the total number of individual votes received by each candidate. Instead, the popular vote is used to calculate the electoral votes for each state. In all but two states, the candidate who wins the popular vote gets all the state's electoral votes. A state's number of US representatives and senators determines its number of electoral votes. There are 538 electoral votes in total. This system was a compromise among the nation's founders. Some wanted the American people to elect the president directly. Others wanted Congress to elect the president. The electoral system gives an edge to less-populated rural states.

Although Clinton lost the electoral vote, she won the popular vote. She got 65,844,610 individual votes, whereas Trump got 62,979,636.[6] The 2016 election was not the first time the popular vote winner lost the presidency. It happened in 1824 to Andrew Jackson, in 1876 to Samuel Tilden, in 1888 to Grover Cleveland, and in 2000 to Al Gore.

nervous, and they woke up a few hours later to the news of Trump's win. Approximately half of them were amazed and delighted. The other half were shocked and crushed. Why was everyone so sure Clinton would win? And why were Clinton supporters so devastated when she lost? The United States had never seen a reaction to election results quite like this one.

By all objective measures, Clinton was highly qualified for the job of US president. She had a long and distinguished career as a lawyer. She was the first woman to become a partner at Rose Law Firm in Little Rock, Arkansas. As First Lady during the two-term presidency of her husband, Bill, she had led his push for health-care reform. She knew exactly what the demands of the presidency were, having lived in the White House for eight years. After that, she served eight years as a US senator for New York, then four years as US secretary of state.[7]

STILL NOT SHATTERED

On the morning of November 9, 2016, Clinton gave a speech conceding the presidential election to Trump. In it, she had a special message for women and girls worried about sexism in the United States. "I know we have still not shattered that highest and hardest glass ceiling, but someday someone will, and hopefully sooner than we might think right now," she said. "And to all the little girls who are watching this, never doubt that you are valuable and powerful and deserving of every chance and opportunity in the world to pursue and achieve your own dreams."[8]

College student Fadumo Osman watches the third presidential debate between Clinton and Trump.

WHAT IS SEXISM ANYWAY?

Sexism is prejudice or discrimination based on a person's gender. Sexism can target anyone. But in the United States, the term usually refers to how people perceive and treat girls and women. It involves believing men and boys can and should do certain things, such as be leaders in business, politics, and academics, while women can and should do a different set of things, such as domestic and caretaking work. Women's abilities and contributions are often valued less than men's.

Trump, in contrast, had no experience in law, government, or any kind of public service. He was a successful businessman and a celebrity. Many experts and ordinary Americans were not sure how Trump's experience would, or even could, translate into the job of president. His behavior on the campaign trail had raised red flags about his character. He had said most Mexican immigrants were violent criminals. He had dismissed the military service of Vietnam War veteran Senator John McCain and the sacrifice of Muslim US Army captain Humayun Khan, who died in the Iraq War (2003–2011). Trump had said false things about historical events, claiming thousands of Muslim immigrants in Jersey City, New Jersey, had cheered as the World Trade Center towers fell on September 11, 2001. He said the only reason Clinton had any success as a presidential candidate was because she played "the woman's card," meaning he believed she won her party's nomination only because she was a woman.[9] He insulted her appearance, her ability, and her integrity. He excused his own bragging about sexual assault as "locker room banter."[10]

Clinton's supporters were appalled that someone as qualified as Clinton could lose to someone who was, they believed, as unqualified—and undignified—as Trump. They concluded sexism must be a key reason for Trump's win. They knew sexism existed in US politics, of course. But they had not realized it was so deeply entrenched. That was a bitter pill to swallow.

The 2016 US presidential election shined a bright light on some difficult questions about US society: How much sexism remains in US politics? How does it affect women's political prospects? How does it play out in legislation on issues that are important to women? What does this mean for the day-to-day lives of all Americans? And what, if anything, should Americans do about sexism in politics?

DISCUSSION STARTERS

- What do you think of the 2016 presidential election result? How did your family or friends react?

- Do you think sexism played a role in the Trump-Clinton race? Why or why not?

- Think of a woman in your life or public life you look up to. What do you admire about her, and why?

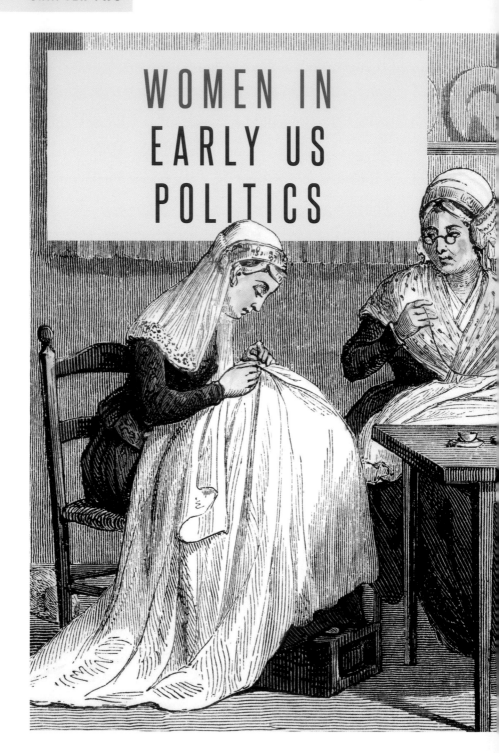

CHAPTER TWO

WOMEN IN EARLY US POLITICS

Women's rights under US law have evolved through the nation's history. Meanwhile, women's representation in US government has also grown. These two developments are tightly intertwined. Gender affects people's experiences in society, and those experiences shape their ideas. People's ideas, in turn, guide public conversation and behavior.

WOMEN'S LEGAL STATUS IN THE NEW NATION

In 1776, the original 13 colonies of the United States of America proclaimed they were breaking away from Britain. The Declaration of Independence was not a description of the United States' government and laws. But it did contain clues about women's legal status in the new nation. In the Declaration, 56 male signers asserted "that all men are created equal, that they are endowed by their Creator with certain unalienable Rights, that among these are Life, Liberty and the pursuit of Happiness."[1] The Declaration also explained that "to secure these rights, Governments are instituted among Men."[2] Back then, it was common to refer to all of humankind as *man* or *men*. Still, the absence of women from the Declaration was telling. Women had very few rights in the early United States—and no representation in its government.

Before the colonies became the United States, their laws were based on the laws of England. These laws said only freeholders could vote. Freeholders were white adult males who owned land worth at least a certain amount of money. The colonists believed this was fair because freeholders paid most of the taxes that supported the government. The colonists thought only freeholders had a serious, permanent interest in the nation's well-being. Colonial laws also said married women could not own property independently of their husbands unless they had signed a special marriage contract agreeing to the ownership. But such contracts were rare and even illegal in some areas. Because most colonial women married, women typically had neither property rights nor suffrage, or voting rights.

However, women were not forbidden outright to vote in colonial America. Some women were single—either unmarried or widowed—and owned land in their own names.

"ONE PERSON IN THE LAW"

From 1765 to 1769, British lawyer William Blackstone wrote a series of books known as *Commentaries on the Laws of England*. These books explained the ideas underlying British law. This quote from Blackstone's *Commentaries* shows how, in Britain and colonial America, women lost their personal legal identities when they married: "By marriage, the husband and wife are one person in the law: that is, the very being or legal existence of the woman is suspended during the marriage, or at least is incorporated and consolidated into that of the husband: under whose wing, protection, and cover, she performs every thing."[3]

AN ACCIDENTAL EXPERIMENT IN WOMEN'S SUFFRAGE

When New Jersey leaders wrote up their state's constitution, they gave voting rights to all inhabitants who were at least 21 years old, owned a certain amount of property, and had lived in the state for one year. And in 1790, a state election law used the phrase "he or she." In 1797, a hotly contested seat in the state legislature brought many New Jersey women to the polls. This started a public debate on women's suffrage. Another hot race in 1806 brought out even more female voters. To end the debate, in 1807, the state legislature changed the word *inhabitants* to *free white men.*

These women could vote in some colonies. One wealthy widow, Lydia Taft of Uxbridge, Massachusetts, did so at least three times. She voted on whether to contribute funds to the French and Indian War (1754–1763) and on taxation and school issues.

When the colonies became states after the American Revolution (1775–1783), each drafted a constitution. This document described the state's basic beliefs and laws, outlined the government's powers and duties, and guaranteed its people certain rights. The states reformed their voting procedures. They all had somewhat different laws, but, generally speaking, they got rid of the freeholder requirement for voting. Instead, they declared all free adult taxpaying male citizens could vote. Women officially had no right to vote. In New Jersey, an opponent of women's voting rights wrote in 1799, "Women, generally, are neither, by nature, nor habit, nor education, nor by their necessary condition in society, fitted to perform this duty [of voting] with credit to themselves, or advantage to the public."[4] Women were not considered fit to vote, and no women held public office. Many men thought the idea of "government in petticoats" was ridiculous.[5]

American independence did not advance American women's political representation. Nor did it advance women's suffrage. But changes to other laws increased women's rights in other areas. Before American independence, when parents died, their property typically went to their oldest son. After American independence was achieved, all the parents' children—including daughters—inherited equal shares of property. Likewise, colonial women had no right to divorce husbands who were abusive, neglectful, or unfaithful. After independence, such divorces were allowed. But none of these newly acquired rights applied to Native Americans or to enslaved women and men forced to

THE US CONSTITUTION

The US Constitution was written in 1787 and approved by the states in 1789. Unlike state constitutions, it does not use the words *men* or *women*, *he* or *she*. Instead, it uses the words *people, persons,* or *electors.* For example, its preamble says, "We the People of the United States, in Order to form a more perfect Union, establish Justice, insure domestic Tranquility, provide for the common defence, promote the general Welfare, and secure the Blessings of Liberty to ourselves and our Posterity, do ordain and establish this Constitution for the United States of America."[6]

Sojourner Truth was an African-American woman who lived from 1797 to 1883. She was born into slavery. She escaped to the farm of an abolitionist family in 1827. Soon thereafter, she became a traveling preacher. In her travels, she met many abolitionists and women's rights activists. She joined both causes. In 1851, she spoke at a women's rights conference in Ohio. In her speech, she described the challenges African-American women faced.

"That man over there says that women need to be helped into carriages, and lifted over ditches, and to have the best place everywhere. Nobody ever helps me into carriages, or over mud-puddles, or gives me any best place! And ain't I a woman? Look at me! Look at my arm! I have ploughed and planted, and gathered into barns, and no man could head me! And ain't I a woman? I could work as much and eat as much as a man—when I could get it—and bear the lash as well! And ain't I a woman? I have borne thirteen children, and seen most all sold off to slavery, and when I cried out with my mother's grief, none but Jesus heard me! And ain't I a woman?"[7]

work on plantations and farms throughout the new country.

ABOLITIONISM AND WOMEN'S RIGHTS

For approximately 50 years, such was the status of American women. Then, it changed again. In the 1830s, thousands of American women became involved in abolitionism, the movement to end slavery in the United States. Abolitionists believed slavery was a moral outrage that needed to end immediately. They pointed to the Declaration of Independence and said the United States should be a haven of freedom for all humankind. They called for emancipating, or freeing, all slaves and assimilating African Americans into US society as citizens. Women in the movement wrote newspaper articles; distributed pamphlets; and circulated, signed, and delivered petitions to Congress calling for abolition. Some women became leaders in the movement.

Though women played a significant role in the abolitionist movement, they faced sexism within the movement. In 1840, the World Anti-Slavery Convention took place in London, England. Prominent US abolitionists Lucretia Mott and Elizabeth Cady Stanton traveled to London to attend the convention. But they were refused seats because they were women. Mott and Stanton vowed to hold their own convention on women's rights.

Sojourner Truth fought for abolition and women's rights.

WOMEN WHO RAN

In 1848, Mott and Stanton held the first women's rights convention in Seneca Falls, New York. The 300 women and men there adopted the Declaration of Sentiments. They modeled this document on the Declaration of Independence to show how American women were deprived of their basic rights. Their declaration demanded the right to vote, the right to equal education, and the right to equal treatment under the law.

Abolitionists and women's rights activists struggled through the 1800s. Some thought ending slavery was more important. Others thought women's rights were more important. Still others fought for both causes. Most women's rights activists suspended their efforts during the Civil War (1861–1865). After the war, the Thirteenth, Fourteenth, and Fifteenth Amendments to the US Constitution respectively abolished slavery, granted citizenship to all people born in the United States, and guaranteed male suffrage regardless of race. But American women would have to wait another 50 years to gain the right to vote nationwide.

In the last decades of the 1800s, most women's rights activists poured their energy into winning the right to vote for women. Through the beginning of the twentieth century, they organized numerous local and state campaigns to persuade politicians to support women's suffrage. As a result, women won the right to vote in Colorado, Idaho, Utah, and Wyoming. Several women ran for public office, and some won, even in states where women could not vote. By 1900, every state had passed laws granting married women some control over their property and earnings.

DISCUSSION STARTERS

- In the 1800s, not all US abolitionists supported equal rights for women. And not all women's rights activists supported the abolition of slavery. Why do you think this was?
- How would you feel if someone refused to acknowledge you simply because of your gender, your skin color, or both?

WOMEN IN TWENTIETH-CENTURY POLITICS

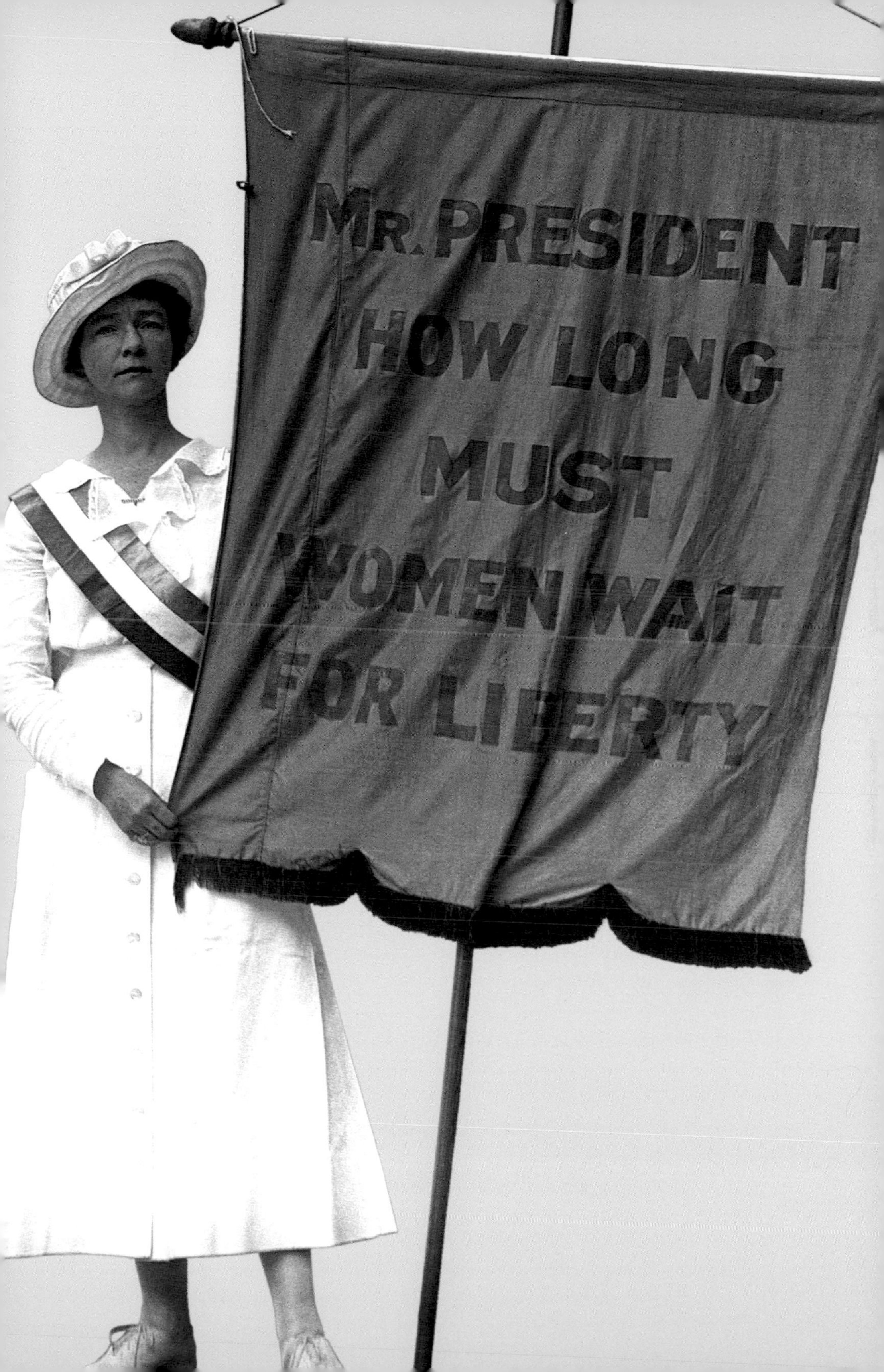
MR. PRESIDENT
HOW LONG
MUST
WOMEN WAIT
FOR LIBERTY

As the 1800s gave way to the 1900s, women's struggle to improve their legal status continued. But after winning the right to vote in four states, the suffrage movement seemed to hit a brick wall. Its original leaders, such as Elizabeth Cady Stanton and Susan B. Anthony, had died. Its members disagreed on who should take the reins and what strategies they should pursue. From 1896 to 1910, no additional states granted women the right to vote. Nonetheless, women's rights activists kept pushing on.

MARCHING TOWARD THE NINETEENTH AMENDMENT

The movement found new energy by welcoming more people into its fold. Among these people were progressive reformers. At the beginning of the 1900s, many American women worked to solve the economic, social, and environmental problems caused by rapid industrialization and mass immigration throughout the country. Many of these issues profoundly affected women at home and in the workplace. Reformers believed the best way to address poverty, racism, and violence was to provide good education, safe environments, and efficient workplaces. They advocated fighting the public's fear of immigrants and exposing the consequences of corporate greed. Reformers urged politicians to let voters decide how to solve problems, and they encouraged Americans to vote. As they tried to convince legislators to pass reform laws, they realized women could be much more persuasive if they had the right to vote a legislator into—or out of—office. So progressive reformers became champions of women's suffrage.

Out of necessity, the women's suffrage movement of the early 1900s also embraced men. All the voters and most of the legislators were men. The movement had to win over men so they would put significant pressure on their fellow voters and legislators. Millions of men did support women's suffrage. Male workers who belonged

Susan B. Anthony, *left,* and Elizabeth Cady Stanton fought for equal rights for US women.

to trade unions were especially strong supporters. They shared many goals with progressive reformers.

In the 1910s, the movement won the vote for women in six more states. Starting in 1913, suffragists began pushing hard for nationwide voting rights. That year, they organized a march calling for an amendment to the US Constitution. They timed the march to coincide with President Woodrow Wilson's inauguration. Eight thousand marchers showed up.[1] They were harassed and assaulted by spectators and police. The marchers' mistreatment became a big news story, which put their cause in the national spotlight. In January 1917, suffragists started continuously protesting in front of the White House. They kept it up six days a week from sunrise to sunset until January 1918, when President Wilson finally gave his support to the Susan B. Anthony Amendment giving women the vote. Wilson said women's suffrage was important to US efforts in World War I (1914–1918). With Wilson's support, the amendment made its way successfully through Congress in 1919. Then, it had to be ratified by three-fourths of the states' legislatures. That finally happened on August 18, 1920.[2]

The Nineteenth Amendment read simply, "The right of citizens of the United States to vote shall not be denied or abridged by the United States or by any State on account of sex."[3] It gave women the right to vote in all elections. As a result, it gave women a say in government. It also provided a legal basis for women to participate in every area of society. Winning suffrage was a turning point for US women, because the right to vote would lead to other rights, too.

MID-CENTURY WOMEN'S RIGHTS

Women's suffrage in the United States opened the door to improvements in all areas of women's rights. However, those improvements did not happen instantly. They took decades of effort—effort that is still under way.

Many suffragists thought winning the vote would quickly bring major changes not only for women, but also for society as a whole. Once the Nineteenth Amendment passed, most suffragists hung up their "votes for women" sashes and focused on other issues. The 1920s turned out to be a decade of unprecedented freedom for women.

JEANNETTE RANKIN

In 1916, Jeannette Rankin, a Montana Republican, became the first woman ever elected to the US Congress. She served in the US House of Representatives from 1917 to 1919, after Montana women gained suffrage but before women won the vote nationwide. She was reelected in 1940 and served from 1941 to 1942. She was the only lawmaker to vote against the United States' entry into both World War I and World War II.

LESER V. GARNETT

When did American women win the right to vote? Was it in June 1919, when Congress passed the Nineteenth Amendment? Or was it in August 1920, when three-fourths of the state legislatures ratified the amendment? Technically, it might be either one of those dates. But practically speaking, it was neither. Women's right to vote was not guaranteed until February 27, 1922, when the US Supreme Court handed down a decision in the case *Leser v. Garnett*.[4]

In October 1920, Cecilia Waters and Mary Randolph of Baltimore, Maryland, registered as voters. Judge Oscar Leser brought a lawsuit against them, saying their names should be removed from the list of voters. He argued that only men could vote according to Maryland's state constitution. The state would have to approve the addition of many more voters to its rolls. Leser also argued that Maryland had not ratified the Nineteenth Amendment. He suggested some of the

Women vote for the first time in New York City in 1920.

states that did ratify the amendment did not have the constitutional power to do so, or they did it incorrectly.

The Supreme Court ruled that the states did in fact have that power, and their ratifications were valid. The court also said the Fifteenth Amendment granting the vote to African-American men had held up constitutionally and so must the Nineteenth Amendment. This decision made sure that women could exercise the right to vote in every state.

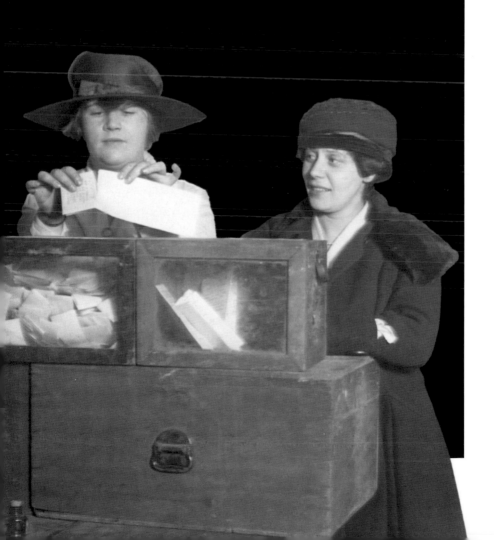

The US economy was flourishing, and many families had cash to spare. They bought devices, such as radios and telephones, that opened up their worlds by delivering new information and ideas from far away. In 1920, a constitutional amendment outlawed alcohol nationwide and began a period called Prohibition. Some women had lobbied hard for Prohibition, believing it would lead to less domestic abuse and loss of income due to drunkenness. A backlash against Prohibition relaxed social norms. Women wore looser, shorter, more comfortable clothing. They gathered in secret bars called speakeasies to drink, dance, and socialize with both women and men.

Some suffragists, however, realized that the fight for women's rights was far from over. Carrie Chapman Catt transformed the National American Woman Suffrage Association into the League of

AFRICAN-AMERICAN SUFFRAGISTS

Many African-American women were active suffragists in the early twentieth century. They joined national suffrage organizations, organized local clubs, and lobbied voters and politicians. Despite their hard work, however, the movement did not fully embrace them. Many suffragists in the South believed only white women should be able to vote. At a large suffrage parade in Washington, DC, in 1913, white organizers asked black marchers, such as writer Ida B. Wells and the women of Delta Sigma Theta sorority from Howard University, to walk in a separate black unit instead of with their state units. Wells refused to do so. And although all women won the vote in 1920, black women quickly lost it due to racial discrimination, especially prominent in the South.

Women Voters to help women across the nation find their political voices through voting. Alice Paul, at the helm of the National Woman's Party, believed suffrage was only the first step toward gender equality. She observed that many US laws treated women differently than men. She wrote the Equal Rights Amendment (ERA) and submitted it to Congress in 1923. It read, "Men and women shall have equal rights throughout the United States and every place subject to its jurisdiction."[5] It was introduced in every congressional session thereafter and was finally voted on in the 1970s.

Despite more freedom in daily life and the ongoing efforts of women's rights activists in the 1920s, social and political equality for women did not change in any concrete or lasting way. Women did not rush out to vote. In fact, they voted at a lower rate than men until the 1950s. And those who did vote often followed their husbands' leads. Women's behavior and their roles in society changed as the nation's fortunes changed. In the 1930s, the Great Depression brought unemployment and poverty to millions of families. Most Americans were simply trying to survive. Few women had the time or resources to be politically active.

In the 1940s, the United States entered World War II (1939–1945) This created a tremendous demand for

Members of the National Women's Political Caucus Gloria Steinem, *left*, Representative Bella Abzug, *standing*, Representative Shirley Chisholm, *center*, and Betty Friedan, *right*, hold a news conference in 1971.

military personnel, equipment, and supplies. Millions of American men of working age fought in the war. Industries struggled to find enough workers to make

the needed equipment and supplies. To keep up with
production, businesses and the government hired millions
of female workers. Society encouraged this as a patriotic

duty. But when World War II ended, the demand for workers fell, and soldiers returned home. Many female workers were fired to make room for the returning men. Female workers were expected to return to—and be happy in—their traditional domestic roles.

WOMEN'S RIGHTS: THE SECOND WAVE

But in the midst of conservative 1950s US society, new ideas were percolating. Women fought for reproductive rights. African Americans began a nonviolent protest movement to reclaim the basic civil rights denied to people of color since shortly after the Civil War. Women in the civil rights movement experienced constant sex discrimination. For example, they were told to march rather than plan marches, to make food for meetings rather than run them, and to hand out literature rather than write it. Meanwhile, French writer Simone de Beauvoir published a book titled *The Second Sex*, urging women to stop defining themselves in relation to other people, such as husbands and children. Instead, she urged female readers to find meaningful careers and seek rights equal to those enjoyed by men. American writer Betty Friedan researched educated women's satisfaction with their lives. Friedan discovered a persistent anxiety and despair that she explained in her book *The Feminine Mystique*. As women digested these ideas and worked in the civil rights movement, many of them realized that to fulfill their own potential and be effective social reformers, they needed to fight for their own rights. The second wave of the women's rights movement had begun.

SHIRLEY CHISHOLM: FIRST AFRICAN-AMERICAN WOMAN IN CONGRESS

Shirley Chisholm was born in New York City to parents who emigrated from Guyana and Barbados. She began her career as an early-childhood educator and administrator. In 1964, she became the second African-American woman elected to New York's state legislature. Four years later, she became the first African-American woman elected to US Congress. In 1972, she was the first African American to run for the presidency. She did not win her party's endorsement, but she did go on to serve a total of seven terms in Congress.

Throughout the 1960s and 1970s, women formed a variety of national and local women's rights organizations.

These groups aimed to change sexist laws and give women and girls equal opportunities in education and jobs. They also encouraged women to become involved in politics and to run for elected office. Through legal battles, lobbying, and public protests, activists achieved several victories. The Equal Pay Act of 1963 required employers to pay women and men equally for equal work. The Civil Rights Act of 1964 outlawed both racial and gender-based discrimination in the workplace. The Higher Education Act of 1972, particularly the amendment known as Title IX, prohibited sex discrimination at any school receiving federal funding.

In 1970, activists revived the ERA. By 1972, thanks to intense lobbying by activists and letters from millions of voters, the ERA sailed through Congress and went on to the states for ratification, quickly racking up approvals.

Then a powerful anti-ERA movement began in 1973, organized by conservative lawyer and activist Phyllis Schlafly.

Women participate in the Women's Equality March and Strike in New York City on August 26, 1970.

She warned that US values and the very fabric of society were at stake. This countermovement ultimately prevented the ERA's ratification before its 1982 deadline. Meanwhile, women grew frustrated with ineffective antidiscrimination laws of the 1960s. Schools and employers continued to discriminate against girls and women, and efforts to right those wrongs were largely ignored by the US government. In addition, second-wave feminism did not adequately include women of color and women in poverty.

WOMEN ON THE US SUPREME COURT

As of 2017, four women have served on the US Supreme Court. They are Sandra Day O'Connor (1981–2006), Ruth Bader Ginsburg (1993–present), Sonia Sotomayor (2009–present), and Elena Kagan (2010–present). In a 2015 interview, Ginsburg said, "People ask me sometimes . . . when do you think it will be enough? When will there be enough women on the court? And my answer is when there are nine."[6] The US Supreme Court consists of nine appointed justices.

Despite these ongoing frustrations, the second wave did have a lasting effect on US law and society. With the legalization of contraceptive pills in 1960 and abortion in 1973, women were better able to decide whether and when to have children. The movement raised awareness of sexual assault and domestic violence and changed the rules of evidence to focus blame on attackers instead of victims. Title IX dramatically increased female participation in sports. And women joined the workforce in large numbers, becoming more prominent in every field.

One of the fields strongly affected by this change was politics. The number of American women in politics has continued to grow. In the 1970s, 1980s, 1990s, and beyond, many women were elected and appointed to state legislatures; the US Congress; judicial seats, including the US Supreme Court; presidential cabinet positions; and more.

DISCUSSION STARTERS

- Abortion rights are a polarizing issue in the United States. People on one side of the argument for or against legalized abortion may have a hard time understanding the other side. Are you on one side or the other? Why? What are some reasons someone might support the other side?

- Do you think amending the US Constitution to include the ERA would be a good idea? Why or why not?

- What do you think Justice Ginsburg meant by her comment about "enough women" on the US Supreme Court? Do you agree or disagree with her? Why?

WHERE WOMEN
STAND TODAY

More than 130 years have passed since Susanna Salter of Argonia, Kansas, became the United States' first female mayor. The same day Salter was elected, women were also voted onto the city council of Syracuse, Kansas. Together, these were the first women elected to any political office in the United States. These events happened in 1887. Since then, American women have made significant progress in politics. However, they are still a long way from achieving parity. Women make up one-half of the US population but nowhere near that fraction of the elected officials in the United States.

THE NUMBERS BY ELECTED OFFICE

The United States is a large country. Its 3.8 million square miles (9.9 million square km) include 50 states plus the District of Columbia and several US territories.[1] As of 2017, the nation was home to approximately 323 million people.[2] There are many political offices up for grabs. In fact, there are more than 500,000 local, state, and federal elected officials in the United States.[3] That figure does not include all the political officials who are appointed by political leaders and not elected by the public, so the real number of political jobs is much larger.

Although detailed, current data are available for state and federal elected offices, data for local elected offices are not as accessible. But the available numbers paint a clear picture: women lag behind men in being elected to public office. A total of 537 elected officials serve in the US federal government. These include the president and vice president, 100 senators, and 435 representatives. As of the 2016 presidential election, no woman has ever served as president or vice president.

Collectively, the US Senate and US House of Representatives are called Congress. Each two-year term of Congress has a name, numbered in ascending order from the 1st Congress in 1789.

TIRED OF WOMEN BEING IGNORED

In 2004, Melissa Hortman won a seat in the Minnesota House of Representatives. Thirteen years later, she had become the House minority leader. Republicans held the majority; Hortman was a Democrat. On April 3, 2017, House members debated a bill that would increase penalties for disruptive protesters. Several female representatives of color rose to speak out against this bill. Meanwhile, a group of white male representatives disappeared into a back room to play cards. Hortman grew frustrated that some of her colleagues were ignoring the female speakers. So she stood up and spoke out: "I hate to break up the 100 percent white male card game in the retiring room," she said, "but I think this is an important debate."[4]

This comment enraged several House Republicans. They said Hortman's comment was racist and sexist. They demanded an apology. Hortman refused. She said, "I'm really tired of watching women of color, in particular, being ignored. So I'm not sorry."[5]

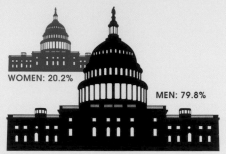

WOMEN: 20.2%

MEN: 79.8%

HOUSE OF REPRESENTATIVES

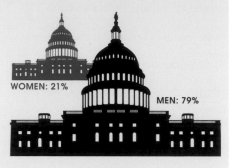

WOMEN: 21%

MEN: 79%

SENATE

Women made up 20.4 percent of the 115th Congress (2017–2019).[6]

Although women have yet to win the presidency and vice presidency and make up only approximately one-fifth of Congress, they have made significant progress. When the US Constitution established the federal government in 1789, there were zero female federal elected officials. The number of women stayed at zero until 1917, when Montana voters sent Jeannette Rankin to Congress. The number grew slowly but steadily—adding a few congresswomen each year—through the 1980s. The 1992 election produced a significant jump from 33 women in the 102nd Congress to 54 women in the 103rd Congress.[7] After that, the number continued to gradually grow to 104 women in the 115th Congress.[8]

In state governments, there are many more elected officials. They include state governors, lieutenant governors, statewide executives, state senators, state representatives, and state judges. In 2017, only six women served as state governors. Women held 22.4 percent of state senate seats and 25.7 percent of state house seats. However, women's representation in state senates and houses had quintupled since 1971.[10] Women were best represented in the state legislatures of Vermont (40 percent), Nevada (39.7 percent), Colorado (39 percent), Arizona (38.9 percent), and Illinois (36.2 percent). Women were worst represented in the state legislatures of Mississippi (13.8 percent), South Carolina (13.5 percent), West Virginia (13.4 percent), Oklahoma (12.8 percent), and Wyoming (11.1 percent).[11]

In 2017 in cities with more than 30,000 residents, 292 of the 1,408 mayors (20.4 percent) were women.[12] Twenty

POLITICAL APPOINTEES

When scholars and journalists talk about women's participation in US politics, they are often referring to elected offices. But winning elections is not the only way to public office. Political appointments are another important way to serve the public. Appointees hold offices from state boards and commissions all the way up to secretaries in presidential cabinets. Appointed offices are often more balanced between the genders than elected offices are. For example, in 2013, state legislators were 22.75 percent women, whereas state appointments were 40.27 percent women.[13]

American women's overall political representation does not match women's representation in the US population. The mismatch is even starker for women of color. Women of color make up approximately 18 percent of the total US population.[16] But only one woman of color served as governor in 2017. In Congress, 7.1 percent of members (36.5 percent of congresswomen) were women of color.[17] US congressional history has seen a total of five women of color in the Senate and 59 in the House.[18]

of the cities with female mayors were among the United States' 100 largest cities.[14]

THE NUMBERS BY POLITICAL PARTY

There is a sharp difference in women's representation between the two major US political parties. There are many more Democratic women serving in elected office than Republican women. In the 115th Congress, women made up nearly one-third (32.2 percent) of the Democratic legislators. By contrast, less than one-tenth (9 percent) of the Republican legislators were women. Since 1981, the number of female Democrats in Congress has grown sixfold. Meanwhile, the number of female Republicans in Congress has stayed relatively constant, growing by only a few women.[15]

The party breakdown for women in state legislatures is similar to that of US Congress. In 2017, women made up more than one-third (35.3 percent) of Democratic state legislators. By contrast, 16.8 percent of Republican state legislators were women.[19]

The party breakdown is different for women in statewide elected executive offices, such as governor. From 1970 to 1990, women in these offices were more likely to be Democrats. But the balance has since shifted. In 2017, women held 75 of 312 available offices.[20] Among these women, 42 were Republicans, 32 were Democrats, and one was not affiliated with a political party.[21]

WOMEN'S REPRESENTATION IN OTHER COUNTRIES

Although the United States is a world leader in many ways, it lags behind other countries in terms of women in politics. The Inter-Parliamentary Union (IPU) is an organization made up of the legislatures and parliaments of all countries. In May 2017, IPU ranked 193 countries by the percentage of women in their legislatures or parliaments. The top two nations were Rwanda (61.3 percent) and Bolivia (53.1 percent). The United States ranked 101st. The bottom four nations were Micronesia, Qatar, Vanuatu, and Yemen (all with 0 percent).[22] Fourteen nations had female heads of government.[23]

DISCUSSION STARTERS

- Are any of your local, state, or national elected leaders women? What is your opinion of them and their job performances? Do you think they face sexism?

- Why do you think women's representation in government has yet to catch up with their proportion of the population?

CHAPTER FIVE

WOMEN RUNNING
FOR OFFICE

Current and historical data clearly show that women are underrepresented in US government and always have been. But those numbers do not show why this is happening. American women have had the vote for 100 years, and their march toward equal rights under US law has been going on even longer. So what is the delay? Many feminists and political researchers have wondered just that. To find the answer, researchers have studied how women and men campaign for office. Researchers have also studied how women fare when they run for office.

WHAT IS FEMINISM?

In simple terms, being a feminist means believing in the political, social, and economic equality of the sexes. But individuals tend to put their own spins—positive or negative—on the definition of *feminism*, and some people oppose feminism. In 1913, British journalist and novelist Rebecca West expressed her frustration with anti-feminism by writing the following in the magazine *Clarion*: "I myself have never been able to find out precisely what Feminism is: I only know that people call me a Feminist whenever I express sentiments that differentiate me from a doormat or a prostitute."[1]

THE GOOD NEWS

Researchers wondered whether women campaign differently than men do. Differences might lead to a different public response in elections. And that, in turn, might explain why there are fewer women in office. But women and men actually campaign very similarly for elected offices in the United States. They raise similar amounts of money.

A New York woman gives her ballot a final look on November 8, 2016.

They run the same numbers of TV commercials. They focus on similar issues, personal traits, and skills in their broadcast media commercials, print advertising, and social media messages.

The public responds to women's and men's political campaigns similarly, too—at least overtly. Media outlets tend to cover campaigns by men and women in equal quantity. Meanwhile, voters respond to these campaigns in a balanced way overall. They say female and male political candidates have similar personal traits and skills. Voters rate candidates of both genders as equally capable on a variety of issues.

This balanced response plays out in voting, too. When women run for office, they win at approximately the same rate as men do. As political science professor Kathleen Dolan points out, "Being a woman doesn't hurt you in an election."[2]

THE BAD NEWS

So if women and men campaign similarly and experience similar success rates in elections, why are so few women in office? There are multiple reasons, but the biggest one plays out even before a campaign or election. It is the decision whether to run for office at all. Far fewer women than men run for elected office. Researchers have uncovered two reasons for this.

Recruitment is the first reason. Women are much more likely to run for office if someone else suggests or encourages it. But political organizations are considerably less likely to recruit women to run for office. This happens even when women are just as professionally qualified and as politically active as their male counterparts. Because men still dominate US politics, the people in charge of recruiting potential candidates are usually men. Men tend to recruit people who are like them: that is, other men.

Ambition is the second reason. When women are recruited for political candidacy,

A RESPONSIBILITY TO KNOW

Jessica Troilo of Morgantown, West Virginia, is one woman who chose not to run for office because of her own high standards. After the 2016 election, she felt inspired to action. She threw her hat in the ring for Morgantown's city council. But she soon felt she was in over her head. She explained, "I didn't want to . . . occupy a position of power where I perceived I had no knowledge. I believe elected officials have a responsibility to know where their constituents live, what their needs are, and what is in their best interests."[3]

they are less likely than men to go ahead with a campaign. Researchers think lingering ideas about traditional gender roles may explain some of this difference. But it is mostly due to other factors. One of these factors is self-judgment. Even when women and men have the same experience, skills, and personal traits, women tend to doubt they are qualified for office. They set a higher standard for themselves than men do. Women are also reluctant to run for office because they see politics as a hostile environment. They fear sexism will lead to unfair treatment by their opponents or the media, in debates, in public conversation, and at the polls.

Pramila Jayapal, *left*, of Washington became the first Indian American to serve in the US House of Representatives when she was sworn in on January 3, 2017.

FEMINIST PARTY FLIP-FLOP

In the 1800s and early 1900s, most women's rights activists supported the Republican Party. The suffrage movement grew from the antislavery movement, and the Republican Party was formed to end slavery. The first US congresswoman was a Republican. A Republican-controlled Congress passed the Nineteenth Amendment. The party continued supporting women's rights through the mid-1900s to grow its numbers. But in the 1960s, it began changing its ideals to win over southerners who opposed racial integration. In the 1980s, the party changed again to win over evangelical Christians who supported traditional gender roles and opposed feminist ideas. Because the Republican Party changed, many feminists changed parties.

THE STORY BEHIND THE NEWS

Modern female candidates do well when they run for political office. But women's persistent lack of recruitment as political candidates, their own reluctance to run for office, and their continuing underrepresentation in government suggest some kind of sexism persists in US politics.

A look at the gender gaps in recent US presidential elections may provide some clues about sexism in politics. Presidential elections tend to bring out more voters than do midterm elections, so they provide a bigger group of nationwide voters to study. An election gender gap is the difference between men's and women's voting habits. For example, in the 2016 presidential election, 41 percent of women voters chose Trump, whereas 52 percent of men did. That's a gender gap of 11 percentage points.[4]

In every presidential election since 1992, women have preferred the Democratic candidate over the Republican one. And during that time, the gender gap has been growing overall. Many experts think this is less about women than it is about men. Women's habits have not changed much in terms of which political party they vote for. Male voters, however, seem to be migrating toward Republican candidates. And evidence suggests that a subtle brand of sexism—"modern sexism"—is one reason why.

The Blair Center Poll is a multiyear survey that examines political behavior and attitudes. So far, the poll has been conducted in 2010, 2012, and 2016. Among other things, it uses a tool called the Modern Sexism Scale (MSS). The MSS

THE MODERN SEXISM SCALE

In the United States today, it is no longer socially acceptable to make directly sexist statements, even if one holds sexist views. This makes it tricky to find out how common sexism is. The MSS measures people's reactions to indirectly sexist statements that express resentment instead of direct prejudice. Participants can respond to each statement by choosing *strongly disagree, disagree, neither/neutral, agree,* or *strongly agree*. Some of the statements include:

- Many women are actually seeking special favors, such as hiring policies that favor them over men, under the guise of asking for "equality."

- Most women interpret innocent remarks or acts as being sexist.

- Feminists are seeking for women to have more power than men.

- When women lose to men in a fair competition, they typically complain about being discriminated against.

- Discrimination against women is no longer a problem in the United States.

tests for resentment toward women using questions about feminism and women in the workplace. The higher the result, the more prevalent sexist attitudes are. In 2016, results of the Blair Center Poll showed a significant difference in sexist attitudes between respondents belonging to the two major political parties. Among Democratic respondents, 21.5 percent scored high on the MSS. Among Republican respondents, 53.3 percent had high MSS scores.[5] Sexism tends to be associated with conservative values and other factors common among Republicans. Yet even Democratic women voted less for Clinton than they had for Democratic male presidential candidates in the past.

DISCUSSION STARTERS

- Have you seen differences in how male and female candidates in political elections campaign or how they are treated by the media? What advantages or disadvantages might a woman have if her campaign is covered differently than a man's by the media?

- Have you seen examples of modern sexism in real life or in the media? Did you recognize them as sexist at the time?

A voter arrives at the voting booth in Nevada, a battleground state, in November 2016.

CHAPTER SIX

MODERN SEXISM
IN US POLITICS

Scientific evidence of modern sexism in US politics is only one part of the picture. To complete the picture, researchers must examine how modern sexism plays out in real life. How does it affect individual perceptions of political candidates? How does it affect voting behavior?

HOSTILE SEXISM: STILL KICKING

Gender-based insults have long been a common way to silence and devalue women in politics. Many historical and modern examples exist. Opponents of suffragists called them ugly. When Victoria Woodhull ran for president in 1872, people called her a "witch" and "Mrs. Satan."[1] In 1887, after Susanna Salter became mayor of Argonia, she received a sexist poem in the mail, along with a drawing of men's pants.

In 1972, when Elizabeth Holtzman first ran for the US House of Representatives, her party's local boss dismissed her and her supporters as "Holtzman and her squaws."[2] *Squaw* is a word for a Native American woman that many consider offensive. When Sarah Palin ran for vice president in 2008, she endured many sexual insults.

TRADITIONAL VERSUS MODERN SEXISM

Sexism is prejudice or discrimination based on a person's gender. That is the simplest definition. But a closer look at sexist speech and behavior shows that different kinds of sexism exist. In the United States, there is both traditional sexism and modern sexism.

Traditional sexism is believing in strict gender roles, such as that women should not work outside the home, or that women should work only as nurses and teachers.

It is believing women are inferior to men. Today, few Americans will say things such as this—either because they do not believe such things or because they know others will find such beliefs unacceptable. Traditional sexism is also known as overt or hostile sexism.

Traditional sexism is a smaller problem in US society than it used to be. Women today have a wide variety of careers. People are exposed to this basic fact and find it more or less normal. Instead, American women today face modern sexism. This is a subtler but equally harmful version of sexism. In a 1937 Gallup poll, 33 percent of Americans said they would vote for a woman for president. In a 2015 poll, 92 percent said they would do that.[3] In the course of eight decades, Americans' stated opinions about women in the presidency changed dramatically, from overtly sexist to overtly nonsexist. But presidential outcomes have not changed at all; Americans still have not elected a woman president. This suggests a hidden form of sexism underlies Americans' behaviors on voting day.

Modern sexism is denying that discrimination against women even exists. It is thinking that women do not have it any harder than men. It is resenting special programs meant to enable more women to become involved in activities they have been discouraged from joining or in

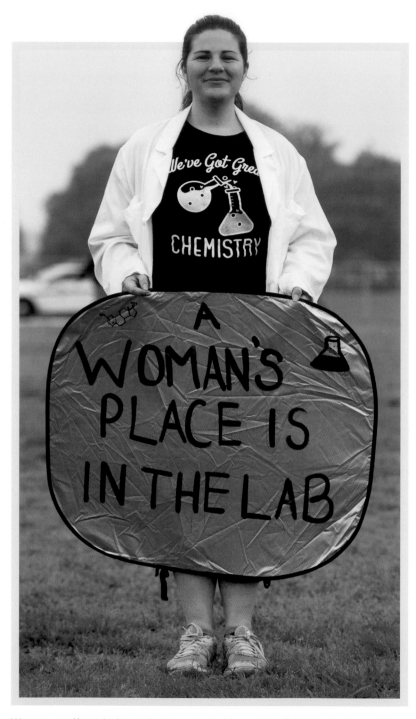

Women continue to be underrepresented in certain fields, including politics and science.

which women are underrepresented, such as science, technology, sports, business, and government. Modern sexism is also known as hidden, invisible, unconscious, ambivalent, or benevolent sexism. It can include behaviors that seem positive toward women, such as men carrying heavy bags for them. But that behavior is based on men feeling superior to women. It can mean men or women having biases against women without even realizing it.

IMPLICIT BIAS

Implicit bias is a key part of modern sexism. Implicit bias is the unconscious tendency to associate certain qualities with certain groups, such as associating women with family and men with careers. Implicit gender bias is internalized sexism.

Implicit bias is hard to measure because it is unconscious. If people do not realize they have a bias, they will not report it. Researchers cannot only ask people questions

REPEAL THE NINETEENTH?

In early October 2016, an interesting public display of political anti-feminism took place on the Internet. It was approximately one month before Election Day. A prominent statistician named Nate Silver shared two maps on Twitter. One map showed that if only men voted in the presidential election, Trump would win handily. The other map showed that if only women voted, Clinton would easily win. These tweets triggered a wave of tweets from Trump supporters calling for a repeal of the Nineteenth Amendment. Many of those tweeting were women.

about their attitudes toward women in various contexts. Instead, researchers need to gauge how strongly people associate women and men with certain ideas. Harvard University scientists ran a ten-year study called Project Implicit. They asked people to sort an array of pictures and words into groups as quickly as possible. The array included gender-related pictures and words such as *man* and *girl* as well as activity-related pictures and words such as *family* and *career*.

TESTING HIDDEN SEXISM

Several different Project Implicit tests are available at https://implicit.harvard.edu/implicit/. Visitors can take these tests to find out about their own unconscious biases. The tests measure biases related to sexuality, age, race, gender and career, religion, weight, mental health, and presidential candidates. Another test called the Ambivalent Sexism Inventory is available at UnderstandingPrejudice.org.

Both Project Implicit's study and a separate study based on the same type of experiment found implicit gender bias varied according to participants' ages, races, sexes, and political leanings. Among other things, the studies showed that regardless of political party or race, women had more implicit gender bias than men. Conservative women were more biased than liberal women.

Among men, conservatives and liberals were almost equally biased. Older people were more biased than younger people.

Implicit bias is difficult to identify.

BIAS IN POLITICS

The effect of implicit gender bias on Americans' behavior at the polls has not been thoroughly studied. But evidence suggests this bias makes a difference in political outcomes generally.

In the first place, implicit gender bias prevents many women from becoming political candidates. As girls

WHAT UNCONSCIOUS SEXISM LOOKS LIKE

In the summer of 2016, the *PBS NewsHour* TV program published an in-depth report on hidden sexism in US politics. An interview within this report showed how an individual may hold both nonsexist and sexist views without even realizing it. The person in question expressed a desire to have a female president someday. But when asked later for views on male and female roles in society, the person replied, "With a man you look for leadership and guidance. With a woman you look for companionship and nurturing. A motherly role."[4]

grow up, they receive more and more exposure to societal ideas about gender roles. And in time, those ideas affect girls' own ambitions. At age seven, equal amounts of girls and boys aspire to be president. But by age 15, far fewer girls than boys feel that way. Political scientists Jennifer Lawless and Richard Fox conducted an analysis to figure out why. In a 2013 report, they identified five reasons: First, parents are more likely to encourage boys than girls to consider a career in politics. Second, girls receive less exposure than boys do—in school, from friends, and through media—to information and discussion about politics. Third, girls are less likely than boys to play organized sports and care about winning. Fourth, girls are less likely than boys to be encouraged to run for office by others. And fifth, girls are less likely than boys to believe that they will someday be qualified to run for political office.

In the second place, implicit gender bias causes women to be judged by their gender in addition to (or instead of) their merits. Significant research has shown that when women seek leadership jobs in business or politics, they must be careful how they act. If women behave in a traditionally masculine way, such as being assertive, competitive, or self-promoting, both men and women find them distasteful. But if women behave in a traditionally feminine way, such as being warm, likeable, and trustworthy, people consider them to be less competent. "You're damned if you do and damned if you don't," says Penn State psychology professor Terri Vescio.[5] For women in politics, there is a double standard. Women are expected to simultaneously act "like women" and act "like men."[6]

DISCUSSION STARTERS

- Take a Project Implicit or Ambivalent Sexism Inventory test. What do you think about your result?

- Why do you think women tend to have more implicit gender bias than men?

- Have you ever thought about pursuing a career in politics? Has anyone ever encouraged you or discouraged you in this line of thinking?

A double standard exists when different groups of people in the same situation are subject to different rules or expectations. The rules might be enforced more strictly for one group than for the other. Or expectations might be completely different for different groups. A sexist double standard exists when people have different expectations or rules for women and men in similar situations. Sexist double standards are common in US politics. Women and men alike tend to have different expectations for female politicians than they have for male politicians. And when the female politicians are women of color, they face an additional set of challenges due to racism.

ON THE ROAD TO PUBLIC OFFICE

Women often encounter double standards on the campaign trail. While they are canvassing neighborhoods to talk to voters, appearing at campaign events, participating in debates, and interacting with journalists, they find themselves being treated differently from their male counterparts. They are asked questions people never ask men. They are judged on criteria that rarely, if ever, apply to men.

Jenny Willford of Colorado once ran for her town's city council. She walked from door to door introducing herself, explaining her vision, and getting to know her neighbors. Every time she went out canvassing, people commented on her appearance and asked her inappropriate questions, such as whether she was married, if her husband approved of her run, and why being a mother to her child was not enough for her.

It is not only candidates themselves who deal with this. Their staff and volunteers do, too. Danielle Corcione, for instance, volunteered for campaign work in college. She was so frustrated by the constant advice on her appearance—"wear glasses to look smarter, and wear brighter clothes to look more feminine"—that she decided against a career in politics.[1]

The media, too, tend to have different expectations for female candidates than for male ones. This is true for media across the political spectrum, from the smallest newspapers to the largest television networks, and for political races from municipal to national. Although media give women and men

COUNTING CALORIES

Presidential candidates on the campaign trail often show up at diners and ice cream parlors. They try the local fare and mingle with voters, hoping to win their support. Reporters usually do not say much about all the food male candidates eat. But they might for a female candidate. During the 2016 presidential campaign, John Kasich stopped at an ice cream shop in Maryland. News stories about that stop covered Kasich's policies and voters' opinions. But a week later, when Hillary Clinton popped into a New York City ice cream shop, a reporter asked her if she knew the calorie count of the treat she had ordered.

roughly the same amount of coverage, the quality of coverage is markedly different.

Media often focus on the gender of female candidates but rarely focus on the gender of male candidates. Studies show media give a lot more attention to female candidates' families, appearances, and personalities than they give to male candidates'. Journalists are particularly hard on female presidential candidates. Their coverage tends to reflect the idea that a president should be male. For example, when Elizabeth Dole sought the Republican nomination in 2000, the media did not take her seriously.

Stories on Dole focused on her appearance, her stiff demeanor, her inadequate fundraising, and the novelty of a female Republican candidate for president. Media treatment of Dole's male competitors was, quite literally, a completely different story. They received more coverage overall, more positive coverage, and no commentary on their gender.

During high-profile political races, candidates sometimes

FAMILY TALK

Candidates and elected officials like to talk about their families. Doing so helps voters see them as ordinary people with ordinary values. But for female candidates, family talk is tricky. They face a dilemma men do not face. If women show voters their families are important to them, voters wonder whether the women will be able to balance their public responsibilities with their private ones. But on the other hand, if women do not mention their families, voters wonder how the women could understand what voters' families need.

agree to debate one another in public or to answer questions at a joint forum. A journalist usually serves as the moderator for a political debate or forum. Moderators tend to hold male and female candidates to different standards. For example, in the series of debates between Clinton and Trump in 2016, observers noticed moderators persistently asked Clinton harder questions than they asked Trump. They also interrupted her more often, and they allowed Trump to interrupt her far more often than they allowed her to interrupt him.

VOTER RESPONSE

A candidate's gender strongly influences how much voters care about the candidate's competence. In a 2016 experiment exploring this issue, Iowa State University political scientist Tessa Ditonto found when she portrayed women and men as competent, they did similarly well in election outcomes and participants' evaluations. But when she portrayed male and female candidates as incompetent, male candidates came out way ahead. In other words, Ditonto found that missteps by women can be fatal, whereas men can get away with making multiple gaffes.

Other political scientists studying voter response to male and female candidates have found similar results. An analysis of past and present research by the nonpartisan organization Political Parity found that even though women who run for office are as likely as men to win, female candidates must be more qualified than male candidates to be successful.

University of Houston political scientist Elizabeth Simas commented on this problem when asked about the 2016 presidential election. She noted, "[Clinton] was faced with complications because there are certain people in this country uncomfortable with a woman taking on this role for the first time. I think we do evaluate female candidates in a different way than we evaluate male candidates. So she probably faced a set of criteria that male candidates don't."[2]

Donald Trump won the 2016 presidential election despite his gaffes during appearances and on social media.

Science shows that when women step outside gender expectations and act like politicians—that is, the same way male politicians act—people judge them differently and more harshly than their male competitors. This double standard dramatically affects who gets elected and thus who gets the power that an elected office provides.

IN OFFICE

Sexist treatment of women in political office is a global problem. In 2016, the Inter-Parliamentary Union (IPU) published a study on the experiences of women in many legislative bodies around the world. The IPU's study found that because women may disrupt a legislature's traditional order, men often resist. Male legislators may challenge their female colleagues' right to be there by making sexist remarks or intimidating or harassing them.

In the United States specifically, when women win elected or appointed office, the double standard they experienced on the campaign trail and on Election Day continues. When women in Congress carry out their jobs by asking difficult questions, raising uncomfortable issues, or being assertive, they often suffer consequences that are not applied to male colleagues who do the same things. This happened to Senator Elizabeth Warren of Massachusetts in February 2017 during the US Senate

US senator Elizabeth Warren speaks with journalists after she was silenced on the floor of the Senate by Majority Leader Mitch McConnell on February 8, 2017.

confirmation hearings for Attorney General Jeff Sessions. Warren started reading aloud a letter from civil rights leader Coretta Scott King. In this letter, King denounced Sessions for having used his position as US attorney for Alabama to keep African Americans from voting. Senate Republicans, a mostly male group, used an obscure rule to cut Warren off. But the next day, when three male senators read aloud from the same letter, no one objected.

A double standard also seems to apply to female politicians when they make mistakes. Observers have noted that when scandals occur in government, the men involved in them suffer fewer consequences than the women do. For example, in December 2011, a group of male state senators in Minnesota revealed that Amy Koch, the state's first female senate majority leader, had had an extramarital affair. This revelation ended her political career. But, as Erin Gloria Ryan, senior editor at *Daily Beast*, points out, many men "have done worse than Amy Koch, and not suffered nearly the professional consequences."[3] It is difficult to scientifically measure the specific effects of double standards on women in politics. But one thing is clear: double standards make the political process a lot harder for women.

NEVERTHELESS, SHE PERSISTED

Senate majority leader Mitch McConnell inadvertently sparked a new feminist slogan with his explanation of why the Senate silenced Elizabeth Warren. The Republican senator said, "Senator Warren was giving a lengthy speech. She had appeared to violate the rule. She was warned. She was given an explanation. Nevertheless, she persisted." Women's rights activists have begun using the last three words of this quote to cheer one another on.[4]

DISCUSSION STARTERS

- Have you ever faced or witnessed a sexist double standard in your school, your extracurricular activities, or your family life?
- Why do you think voters worry about female politicians' ability to balance family and work life when they do not worry about men's ability to do the same thing?

THE EFFECT OF WOMEN IN OFFICE

Despite the obstacles women must overcome to win political office, the sexism they continue to face once they get there, and their persistent underrepresentation, female politicians make a significant difference. They influence the making and enforcement of laws. They bring a variety of tangible benefits to their constituents. And they serve as role models to American girls and women.

LEGISLATION

Female legislators affect lawmaking by bringing attention to issues that are especially important to women, children, and families. These issues include health care, child welfare, environmental protection, reproductive rights, sexual assault, domestic violence, human trafficking, and more. Studies of the US Congress and state legislatures have shown female legislators are more likely to introduce bills on these issues. As bills move through the legislative process, women influence the way in which problems are understood and, therefore, what problem-solving policies are proposed.

Women tend to have different legislative priorities than men because they come to their work having had different life experiences in their education, in their work, and in their home lives. They have personal insight into how health policies affect women. They often have firsthand experience with gender discrimination.

However, the issues female legislators tend to promote are, overall, less likely to succeed than those male legislators promote. Researchers think it is simply a result of fewer women serving in legislatures. To solve this problem, researchers suggest more women should run. And they should serve long enough to earn seniority in their legislatures and have more say on legislative agendas.

UNDERSIZED NUMBERS, OVERSIZED IMPACT

Women make up less than one-quarter of both the US Congress and the state legislatures, but their undersized share of these bodies has an oversized impact on them. Evidence gathered from the entire span of women's legislative history shows women do not need to hold a certain percentage of seats to make a difference in lawmaking. For example, during the 1970s, few women served in Congress. But that is when women's rights under US law improved the most. Women legislators played key roles at key moments to move women's rights legislation forward.

CONSTITUENT BENEFITS

Female legislators bring other benefits in addition to a greater focus on women's, children's, and family issues. Women in Congress consistently perform better than their male colleagues at the two key tasks of legislators. These tasks are lawmaking, or writing bills and shepherding them through the legislative process, and constituent service, which includes bringing federal projects and money to their districts and working directly with constituents.

In 2011, political scientists Sarah Anzia and Christopher Berry published a study of outcomes for US legislative districts from 1984 to 2004. They examined how many federal program dollars members of Congress brought to their home districts. They also examined the lawmaking activities of male and female legislators.

The study found that female legislators bring home an average of 9 percent more federal money than their male colleagues do. Women's districts receive approximately $49 million more per year than men's districts get.[1]

FEMALE POLITICIANS AND "WOMEN'S ISSUES" OVER TIME

Until the twenty-first century, women representatives and senators seemed fundamentally different from their male counterparts. Women were more likely than men to support so-called women's issues. Women in both major parties were more likely than men to sponsor and cosponsor bills focusing on these issues. But as the parties have moved further apart and moderate members have dwindled, party, not gender, now shapes legislators' positions and priorities instead.

Women sponsor and cosponsor more bills than men, and women-sponsored bills garner more cosponsors. Congresswomen have stronger networks of collaboration than congressmen do.

US senator Kamala Harris cheers on California health-care workers at a rally in January 2017.

Congresswomen outperform congressmen for a fairly simple reason: it is hard for women to run for office and become elected. If women think there is gender discrimination in the campaign and election process, or if they underestimate their own qualifications, say Anzia and Berry, "then only the most qualified, politically ambitious females will emerge as candidates." What is more,

FEMALE JUDGES

In 2017, approximately one-third of US Supreme Court justices, federal court of appeals judges, and US district (trial) judges were women. Retired Supreme Court Justice Sandra Day O'Connor and other experts on women in the judiciary say it is important to increase this percentage. They believe that with gender equality among judges, courts will better reflect the population, and people will trust the courts more. They also believe women improve the quality of the US justice system by bringing to it a better understanding of how laws affect girls and women.

they say, "If voters are biased against female candidates, only the most talented, hardest working female candidates will succeed."[2] In other words, sexism in US politics produces outstanding female politicians.

ROLE MODELS

Finally, women in US politics have a positive effect by serving as role models to other American women. When women run for—and win— elected office, women and girls in the general public are more likely to care about and participate in politics. Women and girls are also more likely to be well-informed about political issues when they are represented by women. This effect is stronger in younger women than in older women. It is also stronger when a female politician is a new, well-qualified candidate running for an office currently held by a man. Such candidates inspire more political discussion and action in young women.

One study examined whether prominent female candidates for federal offices, such as Hillary Clinton, Nancy Pelosi, and Sarah Palin—as well as viable female candidates for governor and state senator—had a role-model effect on young women. This study found a role-model effect from former House Speaker Pelosi's election and Clinton's presidential candidacies, but mostly among young Democratic and liberal women. The study found little evidence that Sarah Palin's run for vice president had a similar effect on any young women, regardless of party or ideology. At the state level, the study suggested that female candidates for governor and senator tended to inspire young women who belonged to opposing parties or ideologies.

DISCUSSION STARTERS

- Do you think female leaders in most professions—not only politics, but also education, business, and sports—are usually very well qualified for their jobs? Can you think of some examples?
- Interview your female classmates, friends, or siblings about political role models. Do they feel inspired by women who run for office and win?
- Do you think a more equal gender balance in US government would benefit all Americans or only women? Why?

ACHIEVING PARITY

It is clear that sexism continues to exist in US politics. In a variety of ways, sexism has prevented—and continues to prevent—American women from becoming involved in politics at the same rate as men. It is also clear that having women in US politics brings many benefits—not only to women themselves, but also to their families, their communities, and the nation as a whole. The challenge facing American politics today is how to help American women overcome the political obstacles they face to achieve equal representation in their government.

A DRAMATIC SPIKE

The 2016 US election brought a Republican takeover of both the executive and legislative branches of federal government, as well as Republican wins in many state governments. After the election, a dramatic spike occurred in women's political involvement. This spike was concentrated among women who were Democrats or politically liberal. These women were dismayed by the election of candidates whose agendas, they believed, were sexist and otherwise opposed to progressive ideas on how to govern and improve society.

At the end of April 2017, Emily's List reported it had received inquiries from more than 11,000 women interested in running for political office.[1] Emily's List is an organization whose mission is to recruit and train progressive political candidates as well as to fund their campaigns. Other organizations that train female candidates saw big numbers, too. Nationwide, attendance was way up at these organizations' events. In addition, evidence showed a spike in general political activism among American women. In January, at least four million people showed up for more than 600 women's marches across the United States.[2] A May 2017 survey of 2,000 employed, college-educated adults found 40 percent of its Democratic female participants had signed a political letter or petition in the past six months. That was triple the amount who had done so before the 2016 election. However, no significant change in political activity happened among the Republican women.[3]

The surge in political activity among women is a step toward political parity.

WHY IS PARITY IMPORTANT?

Does it really matter whether women are equally represented in US government? Elizabeth Holtzman thinks so. She is a former US representative, district attorney, and comptroller (chief financial officer) for New York City. She says, "(It) matters not just because an ambitious and qualified woman should be able to advance as far as an ambitious and qualified man, but because politics is about policy. Politics helps determine the kind of society we'd like to live in. And when women are not included in that conversation, or when they're marginalized or drastically underrepresented, it has real-world consequences for our society, for women and our families."[4]

Linda Cavazos, *behind podium*, speaks next to boxes of signed petitions to place gun background checks on the 2016 Nevada election ballot.

But it is only one step. Behind the big numbers lies one number that has not changed: the gender gap in political candidacy. The same survey that showed a spike in political activism also showed women are still less likely than men to actually run for office. Today's women are politically fired up, but men are still twice as likely to seriously consider running for office.

THE BIG PROBLEMS: RECRUITMENT AND AMBITION

Many political scientists who study sexism in politics agree
on two factors that will increase the number of American
women in political office. These factors are improving
recruitment of women and boosting women's political
ambitions. Experts have identified three strategies to
achieve these goals: providing earlier support, giving
more attention to women in local politics, and reframing
politics as a way to serve the public.

HEEDING HER OWN WORDS: LESLIE'S STORY

Leslie Berliant of Cooperstown, New York, is one of the thousands of American women who decided to run for office after the 2016 election. On June 6, 2017, she shared the following with a political support group to which she belongs:

"I went back and read something I wrote the day after the election while thinking about my daughter, a lifelong Hillary fan, and the devastation that she was feeling. 'Here's what I want to say despite feeling utterly shattered: After we mourn we MUST organize. We must be willing to put our skin in the game and be allies, rabble-rousers and loud voices for progress. We must run for local, state, and national office together. We must keep carrying the flames of progress. In the long arc of history, progress always wins. Let's help it along the way.' So a few weeks ago, I decided to heed my own words. I am running for Otsego County Representative, District 7, and I intend to give it everything I've got, for my town, for my county, for my state, for my country and, mostly, for my daughter!"[5]

Women receive the most encouragement late in the political game. Most candidates typically run for national office only after they have gained some experience in local politics. But individuals and organizations give their strongest support to women who have decided to run for a national office. As one analyst explained, that is like trying to put together a good baseball team in game seven of the World Series: impossible. A good baseball team takes years to develop. The same is true for a deep, strong team of female politicians. Women need political encouragement and support much earlier than they're currently receiving it.

When young women receive political encouragement, they are just as likely as young men to respond positively.

Parents are young people's most important influencers. But parents do not equally encourage their daughters and sons to pursue political careers. Parents could help close the gender gap in political ambition by encouraging their daughters more. In addition, young women are less likely than young men to take classes in, read media on, and have discussions about politics. As a result, they feel less knowledgeable about politics. Women's political organizations could address this by becoming more active in middle schools, high schools, and colleges. Schools and communities could also provide girls and young women with more opportunities to play organized sports. These opportunities could build the competitive spirit needed to thrive in politics.

In the United States, there is only one political arena in which women have come anywhere near equal representation. That is the arena of local school boards. Approximately 39,000, or

HOW TO AVOID SEXIST POLITICAL REPORTING

Reducing sexism in the media might help women see the prospect of running for office as a less hostile endeavor. To cover female politicians in a nonsexist way, journalists suggest reporting on a candidate's children, marital status, or appearance only when it is relevant to a policy being discussed or if the candidate brings it up. They should also report on sexist language and gender-based attacks between candidates. The media must be aware of common ideas about gender in US culture and how people express these ideas. Finally, journalists should not pass judgment on a candidate who claims to be the victim of sexism.

43 percent, of the United States' 90,000-plus school board members are women.[6] School board members receive excellent training on how to campaign, raise money, communicate with constituents, and make things happen for their communities. The majority of school board members, both male and female, are open to considering a run for higher office. But the men receive far more encouragement. As a result, few of the women continue on in politics. If political parties recruited more women on school boards to run for higher office, these women could help close the gender gap. "Party members need to be careful of their biases and make sure they're reaching out to women, looking for possible candidates in a variety of settings," says Brigham Young University political science professor Jessica Preece. "And then they need to be

QUOTAS

All the world's countries have some form of sexism. But in 2017, 100 other nations had more female representation in their governments than the United States had. What are those countries doing differently in their political systems? One strategy that several nations use is quotas. They require a certain percentage of political candidates or legislators to be women. This strategy does increase women's participation in politics but with mixed results. For example, in Brazil, political parties often only recruit female candidates to comply with quotas, not in a serious effort to elect them. By contrast, in Rwanda, quotas have brought a dramatic increase in women's election to public office as well as new laws on gender-based violence, women's property rights, and women in the workforce.

sure they're specific about how they're going to help throughout the process."[7]

When political parties do decide to recruit women, a new approach to recruitment might be effective in drawing in female candidates. Studies have found that when political careers are presented to be mostly about having power, men respond more enthusiastically than women do. But when political careers are presented as a way to solve problems and improve communities, both women and men respond enthusiastically. If political recruiters focus on how politicians can work together to make the world a better place, they might be able to recruit more service-minded men as well as more women.

LOOKING FORWARD

Even though women have come a long way in US politics, they have a long way to go. According to Jennifer Lawless, "There's no question that there's been progress over the past century. But before [Jeannette] Rankin would tell us to pat ourselves on the backs for all we've accomplished, she might also remind us that at this rate, it'll take another 100 years to approach any semblance of gender parity in numeric representation."[8]

Public perceptions of women in politics are complex. They depend heavily on individual life experiences,

Encouraging young women and girls to participate in politics can help break down biases.

age, environment, and similar factors. Traditional ideas about gender roles persist. They are not quickly or easily changed. "But," says Elizabeth Simas, "I think the more women we can get into lower offices, the more comfortable people will become with the idea of female leaders and I think some of these implicit biases can be broken down."[9] The surest route to political parity is a slow and steady one: actively encouraging girls in political learning activities and actively recruiting women for political office. The more women who run for—and win—public office, the more everyone sees that politics is for everyone.

DISCUSSION STARTERS

- What classes or clubs about politics and government for young people does your school or community offer?

- How many members of your local school board are men? How many are women? What effects do you think the gender balance has on your district?

- Do you think political quotas are a good idea for the United States? Why or why not?

ESSENTIAL FACTS

SIGNIFICANT EVENTS

- In 1848, Elizabeth Cady Stanton and Lucretia Mott held the United States' first convention on women's rights in Seneca Falls, New York. Three hundred women and men discussed, adopted, and signed the Declaration of Sentiments, demanding a variety of rights for women.

- Jeannette Rankin became the first woman elected to the US Congress in 1916.

- On August 18, 1920, the Nineteenth Amendment, granting women the right to vote, was officially ratified by three-fourths of US state legislatures.

- Sandra Day O'Connor became the first woman to be appointed to the US Supreme Court in 1981.

- In July 2016, Hillary Clinton became the first woman in US history to win the presidential nomination of a major political party. She went on to win the popular vote but lost the electoral vote.

KEY PLAYERS

- Susan B. Anthony was an activist for abolition of slavery and women's rights. She and Elizabeth Cady Stanton led the women's rights movement from 1851 until Anthony's death.

- Hillary Clinton was the first woman to become a partner at the prestigious Rose Law Firm in Little Rock, Arkansas. She was First Lady of Arkansas when her husband, Bill, was governor, and she became First Lady of the United States during her husband's two-term presidency. She also served eight years as a US senator for New York, then four years as US secretary of state.

- Phyllis Schlafly was a US lawyer and conservative activist known primarily for founding the STOP ERA movement.

- Elizabeth Cady Stanton was an abolitionist and women's rights activist. She and Lucretia Mott founded the organized women's rights movement in the United States.

IMPACT ON SOCIETY

Engaging in politics is one of the main ways people can exercise power within US society. Women are drastically underrepresented in US politics and, as a result, their interests, perspectives, and skills are underrepresented in government decision-making.

QUOTE

"Women, especially young women, still face substantial obstacles in the political sphere. Right now, of the 435 members of the House, only 84 are women; in the 100-member Senate, just 20 are women. And that matters not just because an ambitious and qualified woman should be able to advance as far as an ambitious and qualified man, but because politics is about policy. Politics helps determine the kind of society we'd like to live in. And when women are not included in that conversation, or when they're marginalized or drastically underrepresented, it has real-world consequences for our society, for women and our families."

—*Elizabeth Holtzman, June 29, 2016*

GLOSSARY

ABOLITIONIST

A person who wants to end slavery.

CABINET

A group of people whose job is to advise the head of a government, such as a president.

CIVIL RIGHTS

A guarantee of equal social opportunities and equal protection under the law, regardless of gender, race, religion, or other personal traits.

CONSERVATIVE

A person who believes in small government and established social, economic, and political traditions and practices.

CONSTITUENT

A voter or resident of an area who is represented by an elected official.

CONSTITUTION

The basic beliefs and laws of a nation or state that establish the powers and duties of the government and guarantee certain rights to the people in it.

DISCRIMINATION

Treating some people better than others without any fair or proper reason.

LIBERAL

A person who believes in large government and supports new ideas and ways of behaving.

LOBBY

To try to influence public officials.

PARITY

Equality.

PARLIAMENT

A nation's legislature, usually made up of elected representatives.

REFERENDUM

A vote the general public takes on a single political question.

TRADE UNION

An association of workers who negotiate with employers over wages, benefits, and working conditions.

ADDITIONAL RESOURCES

SELECTED BIBLIOGRAPHY

"The Women's Rights Movement." *American Social Reform Movements Reference Library*, edited by Carol Brennan, et al., vol. 2: Almanac, UXL, 2007. Web. *Gale: US History in Context*. 25 Sept. 2017.

Bush, Daniel. "The Hidden Sexism That Could Sway the Election." *PBS NewsHour*. NewsHour Productions, 2016. Web. 16 May 2017.

"Milestones for Women in American Politics." *Center for American Women and Politics*. Center for American Women and Politics, 2016. Web. 17 May 2017.

"Women in Government." *Catalyst*. Catalyst, 15 Feb. 2017. Web. 6 June 2017.

FURTHER READINGS

Adichie, Chimamanda Ngozi. *We Should All Be Feminists*. New York: Anchor, 2015. Print.

Archer, Jules. *The Feminist Revolution: A Story of the Three Most Inspiring and Empowering Women in American History: Susan B. Anthony, Margaret Sanger, and Betty Friedan*. New York: Sky Pony, 2015. Print.

Cooper, Ilene. *A Woman in the House And Senate: How Women Came to the United States Congress, Broke Down Barriers, and Changed the Country*. New York: Abrams, 2014. Print.

Kops, Deborah. *Alice Paul and the Fight for Women's Rights: From the Vote to the Equal Rights Amendment*. Honesdale, PA: Calkins Creek, 2017. Print.

ONLINE RESOURCES

Booklinks
NONFICTION NETWORK
FREE! ONLINE NONFICTION RESOURCES

To learn more about sexism in politics, visit **abdobooklinks.com**. These links are routinely monitored and updated to provide the most current information available.

MORE INFORMATION

For more information on this subject, contact or visit the following organizations:

GIRLS IN POLITICS
655 15th Street NW
Washington, DC, 20005
202-660-1457 ext. 2
girlsinpolitics.org

Girls in Politics (GIP) is a program sponsored by the Political Institute for Women. GIP introduces girls ages eight to fifteen to politics, policy, the US Congress, parliaments, and the work of the United Nations.

RUNNING START
1310 L Street NW, Suite 820
Washington, DC, 20005
202-223-3895
runningstartonline.org

By educating young women and girls about the importance of politics and by teaching them the skills they need to be leaders, this organization gives women the running start they need to achieve greater political power.

SOURCE NOTES

CHAPTER 1. "THAT HIGHEST AND HARDEST GLASS CEILING"

1. Hillary Clinton. "Text of Clinton's 2008 Concession Speech." *Guardian*. Guardian News & Media, 7 June 2008. Web. 18 May 2017.

2. Brian Stelter. "In Their Own Words: The Story of Covering Election Night 2016." *CNN*. Cable News Network, 5 Jan. 2017. Web. 18 May 2017.

3. "Statistical Overview of Women in the Workforce." *Catalyst*. Catalyst, 10 May 2017. Web. 19 May 2017.

4. Susan G. Hauser. "The Women's Movement in the '70s, Today: 'You've Come a Long Way,' But . . . " *Workforce*. Workforce Magazine, 15 May 2012. Web. 19 May 2017.

5. Jonathan Webb. "Glass Ceiling Still Keeps Top Jobs for the Boys: Women Earn 75 Percent of Men's Salary." *Forbes*. Forbes, 30 Jan. 2017. Web. 19 May 2017.

6. David Wasserman. "2016 Popular Vote Tracker." *Cook Political Report*. Cook Political Report, 3 Jan. 2017. Web. 24 May 2017.

7. Betty Boyd Caroli. "Hillary Clinton." *Encyclopaedia Britannica*. Encyclopaedia Britannica, 28 Mar. 2017. Web. 18 May 2017.

8. Hillary Clinton. "Hillary Clinton's Concession Speech: Full Transcript." *Guardian*. Guardian News & Media, 9 Nov. 2016. Web. 18 May 2017.

9. Tamara Keith. "Sexism Is Out in the Open in the 2016 Campaign. That May Have Been Inevitable." *NPR*. NPR, 23 Oct. 2016. Web. 18 May 2017.

10. Pamela B. Paresky. "What's Wrong with Locker Room Talk?" *Psychology Today*. Sussex Publishers, 10 Oct. 2016. Web. 19 May 2017.

CHAPTER 2. WOMEN IN EARLY US POLITICS

1. "Declaration of Independence: A Transcription." *NARA*. Office of the Federal Registrar, 19 Jan. 2017. Web. 26 May 2017.

2. Ibid.

3. Marylynn Salmon. "The Legal Status of Women, 1776–1830." *Gilder Lehrman Institute of American History*. Gilder Lehrman Institute of American History, 2017. Web. 26 May 2017.

4. "Who Voted in Early America?" *Constitutional Rights Foundation*. CRF, 2017. Web. 30 May 2017.

5. Ibid.

6. "The Constitution of the United States: A Transcription." *NARA*. Office of the Federal Registrar, 28 Feb. 2017. Web. 31 May 2017.

7. Paul Halsall. "Modern History Sourcebook: Sojourner Truth: 'Ain't I a Woman?', December 1851." *Fordham University*. Fordham University, 1997. Web. 10 Jul. 2017.

8. "Milestones for Women in American Politics." *Center for American Women and Politics*. CAWP, 2016. Web. 17 May 2017.

CHAPTER 3. WOMEN IN TWENTIETH-CENTURY POLITICS

1. Alan Taylor. "The 1913 Women's Suffrage Parade." *Atlantic*. Atlantic Monthly Group, 1 Mar. 2013. Web. 2 June 2017.

2. "WWI and Winning the Vote." *National Women's History Project*. National Women's History Museum, 2007. Web. 2 June 2017.

3. "Transcript of 19th Amendment to the US Constitution: Women's Right to Vote (1920)." *Ourdocuments.gov*. NARA, n.d. Web. 2 June 2017.

4. Lily Rothman. "How a Little-Known Supreme Court Case Got Women the Right to Vote." *Time*. Time, 27 Feb. 2015. Web. 14 June 2017.

5. Roberta W. Francis. "The History behind the Equal Rights Amendment." *Equal Rights Amendment*. Alice Paul Institute, n.d. Web. 5 June 2017.

6. Gwen Ifill. "When Will There Be Enough Women on the Supreme Court? Justice Ginsburg Answers That Question." *PBS NewsHour*. NewsHour Productions, 5 Feb. 2015. Web. 5 June 2017.

CHAPTER 4. WHERE WOMEN STAND TODAY

1. "State Area Measurements and Internal Point Coordinates." *US Census Bureau*. US Department of Commerce, 2010. Web. 6 June 2017.

2. "Annual Estimates of the Resident Population: April 1, 2010 to July 1, 2016." *US Census Bureau*. US Department of Commerce, n.d. Web. 6 June 2017.

3. Jennifer L. Lawless. *Becoming a Candidate: Political Ambition and the Decision to Run for Office*. New York: Cambridge UP, 2012. Print. 33.

4. Briana Bierschbach. "Melissa Hortman Still Isn't Sorry." *MinnPost*. MinnPost, 26 Apr. 2017. Web. 6 June 2017.

5. Ibid.

6. "Women Representatives and Senators by Congress, 1917–Present." *History, Art, & Archives of the United States House of Representatives*. Office of the Historian, 2017. Web. 17 Aug. 2017.

7. Jennifer E. Manning. "Women in Congress: Historical Overview, Tables, and Discussion." *Congressional Research Service*. CRS, 29 Apr. 2015. Web. 6 June 2017.

8. "Women in Government." *Catalyst*. Catalyst, 15 Feb. 2017. Web. 6 June 2017.

9. Ibid.

10. Ibid.

11. Kelly Dittmar. "Women in State Legislatures 2017." *Center for American Women and Politics*. CAWP, 17 Jan. 2017. Web. 6 June 2017.

12. "Women Mayors in US Cities 2017." *Center for American Women and Politics*. CAWP, 2017. Web. 6 June 2017.

13. Kaitlin Sidorsky. "From Ballot to Binder: How Women in Political Appointments Tell a Different Story of Political Ambition Than Women in Elected Office." *LSE Research Online*. London School of Economics and Political Science, 2015. Web. 6 June 2017.

14. "Women in Elective Office 2017." *Center for American Women and Politics*. CAWP, 2017. Web. 6 June 2017.

15. Kelly Dittmar. "Women in the 115th Congress." *Center for American Women and Politics*. CAWP, 3 Jan. 2017. Web. 6 June 2017.

16. Judith Warner. "Fact Sheet: The Women's Leadership Gap." *Center for American Progress*. Center for American Progress, 7 Mar. 2014. Web. 10 Jul. 2017.

17. "Women in Government." *Catalyst*. Catalyst, 15 Feb. 2017. Web. 6 June 2017.

18. "History of Women of Color in US Politics." *Center for American Women and Politics*. CAWP, 2017. Web. 6 June 2017.

SOURCE NOTES
CONTINUED

19. Kelly Dittmar. "Women in State Legislatures 2017." *Center for American Women and Politics*. CAWP, 17 Jan. 2017. Web. 6 June 2017.

20. "Women in Statewide Elective Executive Office 2017." *Center for American Women and Politics*. CAWP, 2017. Web. 6 June 2017.

21. Ibid.

22. "Women in National Parliaments." *Inter-Parliamentary Union*. Inter-Parliamentary Union. 1 June 2017. Web. 6 June 2017.

23. "Women in Government." *Catalyst*. Catalyst, 15 Feb. 2017. Web. 6 June 2017.

CHAPTER 5. WOMEN RUNNING FOR OFFICE

1. Rebecca West. "Mr. Chesterton in Hysterics: A Study in Prejudice." *Clarion*. Marxists.org, 14 Nov. 1913. Web. 7 June 2017.

2. Maggie Koerth-Baker. "Why We Don't Know How Much Sexism Is Hurting Clinton's Campaign." *FiveThirtyEight*. FiveThirtyEight, 5 Nov. 2016. Web. 17 May 2017.

3. Jessica Troilo. "Why I Didn't Run for Office . . . This Time." *Five Minutes*. Five Minutes, 11 Mar. 2017. Web. 7 June 2017.

4. "The Gender Gap: Voting Choices in Presidential Elections." *Center for American Women and Politics*. CAWP, 2017. Web. 6 June 2017.

5. Angie Maxwell and Todd Shields. "The Impact of 'Modern Sexism' on the 2016 Election." *Diane D. Blair Center of Southern Politics and Society*. University of Arkansas, 2017. Web. 7 June 2017.

CHAPTER 6. MODERN SEXISM IN US POLITICS

1. Elizabeth Holtzman. "'Not a Job for a Woman.'" *Politico Magazine*. Politico, 29 June 2016. Web. 13 June 2017.

2. Daniel Bush. "The Hidden Sexism That Could Sway the Election." *PBS NewsHour*. NewsHour Productions, 2016. Web. 16 May 2017.

3. Jessica Valenti. "Why Are Top Women Politicians Still Peppered with Gender-Specific Slurs?" *Guardian*. Guardian News & Media, 28 Dec. 2015. Web. 7 June 2017.

4. Daniel Bush. "The Hidden Sexism That Could Sway the Election." *PBS NewsHour*. NewsHour Productions, 2016. Web. 16 May 2017.

5. Ibid.

6. Ibid.

CHAPTER 7. DOUBLE STANDARDS

1. Jillian Richardson. "Sexism in Politics: 10 Women Share Their Stories." *Teen Vogue*. Conde Nast, 18 Oct. 2016. Web. 17 May 2017.

2. Eric Fish. "How 'Modern Sexism' Influences American Politics." *Asia Society*. Asia Society, 25 Jan. 2017. Web. 16 May 2017.

3. Erin Gloria Ryan. "Cheating Men Get a Second Life in Politics, Cheating Women Get a Scarlet Letter." *Daily Beast*. Daily Beast, 30 Nov. 2016. Web. 7 June 2017.

4. Somya Jain. "Mitch McConnell's Treatment of Elizabeth Warren Reveals Double Standards in American Politics." *Odyssey*. Odyssey Media Group, 9 Feb. 2017. Web. 7 June 2017.

CHAPTER 8. THE EFFECT OF WOMEN IN OFFICE

1. Sarah Anzia and Christopher Berry. "The Jackie (and Jill) Robinson Effect: Why Do Congresswomen Outperform Congressmen?" *Goldman School of Public Policy*. University of California, Berkeley, May 2010. Web. 12 June 2017.

2. Ibid.

CHAPTER 9. ACHIEVING PARITY

1. Tom Embury-Dennis. "Donald Trump Has Inspired More Than 11,000 Women to Consider Running for Political Office." *Independent*. Independent, 25 Apr. 2017. Web. 17 May 2017.

2. Amanda Ripley. "What It Will Take for Women to Win." *Politico Women*. Politico, 12 June 2017. Web. 13 June 2017.

3. Jennifer L. Lawless and Richard L. Fox. "The Trump Effect." *American University School of Public Affairs*. American University, June 2017. Web. 13 June 2017.

4. Elizabeth Holtzman. "'Not a Job for a Woman.'" *Politico Magazine*. Politico, 29 June 2016. Web. 13 June 2017.

5. Leslie Berliant. *Facebook*. 6 June 2017. Web. 13 June 2017.

6. Amanda Ripley. "What It Will Take for Women to Win." *Politico Women*. Politico, 12 June 2017. Web. 13 June 2017.

7. Emma Cueto. "Why Don't More Women Run for Political Office? This Study Shows That Changes in the Recruitment Process Are Needed." *Bustle*. Bustle, 12 Oct. 2016. Web. 13 June 2017.

8. Jennifer Lawless. "Congress 100 Years Later: What Would Jeannette Rankin Think?" *Vox*. Vox, 6 Apr. 2017. Web. 17 May 2017.

9. Eric Fish. "How 'Modern Sexism' Influences American Politics." *Asia Society*. Asia Society, 25 Jan. 2017. Web. 16 May 2017.

INDEX

ABOUT THE AUTHORS

DUCHESS HARRIS, JD, PHD

Professor Harris is the chair of the American Studies Department at Macalester College. The author and coauthor of four books (*Hidden Human Computers: The Black Women of NASA* and *Black Lives Matter* with Sue Bradford Edwards, *Racially Writing the Republic: Racists, Race Rebels, and Transformations of American Identity* with Bruce Baum, and *Black Feminist Politics from Kennedy to Clinton/Obama*), she has been an associate editor for *Litigation News*, the American Bar Association Section's quarterly flagship publication, and was the first editor-in-chief of *Law Raza Journal*, an interactive online race and the law journal for William Mitchell College of Law.

She has earned a PhD in American Studies from the University of Minnesota and a Juris Doctorate from William Mitchell College of Law.

CHRISTINE ZUCHORA-WALSKE

Christine Zuchora-Walske has been writing and editing books and articles for children, parents, and teachers for 25 years. Her author credits include books for children and young adults on science, history, and current events; books for adults on pregnancy and parenting; and more.